LOVE AROUND THE WORLD

LOVE AROUND THE WORLD

Relationship Traditions Across Cultures

AVERY NIGHTINGALE

QuantumQuill Press

CONTENTS

1	Introduction	1
2	Western Traditions	2
3	Eastern Traditions	6
4	African Traditions	10
5	Middle Eastern Traditions	14
6	South American Traditions	18
7	Asian Traditions	23
8	European Traditions	27
9	Oceanic Traditions	31
10	Conclusion	35

Copyright © 2024 by Avery Nightingale

All rights reserved. No part of this book may be reproduced in any manner whatsoever without written permission except in the case of brief quotations embodied in critical articles and reviews.

First Printing, 2024

CHAPTER 1

Introduction

We wanted to have the whole world within the limits of modern society. And we've created something like that. We've crossed borders in a moment and traveled all over the world where love lived as an indivisible and eternal feeling. Does love have boundaries between countries, religions, and nations? A person is born on this planet, becomes a citizen of a certain country, and starts to understand not always correctly. That's why some confine themselves to what was established before and had been accepted as a tradition in world society.

Even ancient people fall in love. Be sure, we are not trying to offend your cognitive abilities at all. Nevertheless, the very notion that love exists, distinguishes from friendship and family types of relationships, and is the last link in the strength chain of bonds that lead to happy and cloudless marriage aspirations, is not so old and has changed over the long time of human existence. The history of the concept of love began more than 2,500 years ago. Now we are treating the theme of love in our project. Let's discover love in world traditions, exploring the traditions of different cultures, to find all the sample beauty and complexity of diverse forms of human relationships within the world's veil.

CHAPTER 2

Western Traditions

After several months or years of dating, a couple decides to make their nuptials "official" by wearing wedding rings. There are many traditions behind wedding rings, though, and what they symbolize has varied over the centuries. For the ancient Greeks and Romans, a simple gold band represented a verbal contract from the groom's family and acceptance by the bride's parents that the couple in question formed a lawful and recognized marriage. It was also said that the third finger on the left hand was known as the "vena amoris," or the vein of love, which was said to run from the third finger directly to the heart. Therefore, the act of wearing an engagement and wedding ring on that particular finger signified to the couple and those around them that they were bound heart and soul by law and love. Over time, beliefs have changed, but despite the fear of the "bad luck finger," this tradition has survived —and in various forms around the globe!

Throughout Europe, double wedding bands have borne a variety of inscriptions, each indicating that the recipient wearer is loved and cherished by the gift-giver. In late 17th century Europe, it was more or less decided that these inscriptions would be in the form of a verse, while others took the form of a poem. Regardless of the inscription's form, though, any ring from the man to the woman representing lasting adoration would speak volumes. The key to understanding the meaning of the double wedding band is the Ring King, or Gimmel. A Gimmel ring, derived from the Latin gemellus, or twin, is composed of two or three rings that fit together like a puzzle. The "puzzle" is made up of two pieces of metal or stone, and when separated, they form two or three individual rings. Long used as a pre-engagement or engagement symbol, over time, when this phrase was separated, the concept of a shared eternally inscribed wedding band for the man and woman remained ever present, if only in one ring.

2.1. Dating Culture

The cultural differences in the types of relationships don't just end at the point of defining them. You can be dating an African and the first time you meet his/her family, they will naturally assume you're getting married. Relating this to another key cultural difference, we can highlight Indian dating culture. While in India dating is more about getting to know each other without a permanent commitment, in many Middle Eastern societies (especially, but not limited to Indian), an unmarried couple doesn't walk down the street without derogatory stares and no room for any PDAs. However, parents' involvement with their children's dating is not a strictly Middle Eastern custom. While living in China, I bumped into many middle-aged singletons at those occasional matchmaking corner hangouts in different cities across China. In many Vietnamese families, children can get really uncomfortable with their parents and even grandparents questioning them about why they haven't got hitched yet. Curious occurrences don't stop on the mainland!

Growing up in Europe, at least having traveled around for a bit, I had never encountered the western approach to dating as it happens in the US, the UK, and Australia. To be aggressive in dating is a very weird command! Despite the globalization and level of departure that stands from the American heritage (which everybody in the world wants to adopt or admire), culturally, the more people of the less romantic cultures integrate the purely western concept of dating, the more unique these up-to-now behaviors keep feeling on the widespread territories on our planet. These unspoken, unwritten things one must do or what one must expect from their partners and the world, in this feverish race of self-inclusion and the 'self-reclaiming' practices, an equality has much room for improvement, not only in women's health rights but also in the exposure of the anxiety issues and restrictions regarding different typologies of men.

2.2. Marriage Customs

Common-law marriages are also common around the world, along with marriage by cohabitation and even smaller formalities. In Canada, common-law unions have been on the rise, with the number of common-law couples having increased by 14.5% from 2006 to 2011. In other cultures, cohabitation is favored, as in Mexico, Denmark, Belgium, Sweden, and Norway. From Asia and the Middle East, the custom of Misyar marriages in Saudi Arabia, Sigheh and Chādor Bāzī in Iran, fixed-term marriages, and in some Pakistani societies, the custom of woman-watta are various forms of temporary marriage, pursued by followers of Islam. Throughout much of history, and even until present, families arranged marriages at the discretion of both parents and/or the couple. In China, dating is discouraged early in a woman's life, and the woman is advised to focus on school, avoiding romantic entanglements until around age 20. In India, arranged marriages are considered the tradition.

Another custom is the son-in-law who regularly resides in the house of his wife's family to take care of their parents-in-law. The Ndawara people arrange harpagopharies marriages, in which a wife is married to a "foreign man" to avoid conflict. These unions are considered "officially" polyandrous in the eyes of the law, but they are rarely practiced today. Another form of marriage, often referred to as levirate marriage whereby a woman is wed to her deceased sibling's husband, is prominent within the Zulu culture of South Africa. If the two are related in the same way, they will simply have a vambúneo (informal union). This ritual is thought to purify the couple, and it is believed that it ensures good fortune. During a macosa marriage, the groom will leave one of his own to give it to the bride, which is thought to strengthen the marriage. In some cultures, the duration of time a newlywed bride is taken away from the groom post-ceremony is varied.

2.3. Gender Roles

In North America, the traditional roles of gender within committed relationships were that children should have two parents and that one parent should work while the other should stay at home and raise the children full time. Over time, people have strengthened and put more progressive gender roles in place, where both parents take active roles in raising and providing for the kids. However, in some families, including his, these traditional roles are still in place. When a man is engaged, the couple is considering people in the United States to be a team and treat everything they do as a partnership.

In New Zealand, the traditional roles of gender were evident in the sample. New Zealanders have liberal gender ideologies and a work-life balance, and the data suggested for the sample studied that those ideologies are generally held. Nora, Emma, and Tori's partners often worked fewer hours so they could raise their children, and they were responsible solely for the family's financial care needs. Additionally, Felicity's parents practiced traditional gender roles and she pointed to them as the reason she and her partner were trying to resist those roles.

It is important to recognize that tradition may be difficult to change, as children of people who opposed traditional gender roles carried their ideology into their own families. In that light, it is also reasonable to recognize that gender roles may become a tradition that is difficult, but not impossible, to change. People may recognize practices as part of their tradition but still make efforts to resist those practices. The traditional gender roles that students reported were not results of their setting in New Zealand alone. They were practices that were attentive to common being in several different countries. It is possible that the theorized connection between gender roles and the tradition in society is significant and worth considering in future studies, across disciplines.

CHAPTER 3

Eastern Traditions

India is a vast, diverse country with a complex array of languages, cultures, and traditions. Over 80% of Indians practice a form of Hinduism. At the time of this writing, that's a whopping 1.08 billion people. The Indian population, currently at 1.35 billion, is the second fastest growing in the world after China. Lavish, ornate temples to Hindu deities dot the Indian landscape, both in urban areas and preeminent among the natural beauty of the subcontinent. Interest in romantic love is an ancient part of the Hindu tradition, and a frequent metaphor for the divine is the romantic interactions of gods with goddesses. Certainly, the religious literature of India has celebrated love and romantic relationships for centuries. But traditionally, in Indian "arranged marriages," the primary relative was not the mother-in-law or the cousin, but the husband or the wife.

In an "arranged couple," some self-selection is still operating. Marrying mostly within their endogamous communities, suitable partners were identified for brides and grooms based on moral values, astrological compatibility, social networks, income, caste, age, dietary patterns of the groom, and other legal and religious issues. These traditions have eroded a great deal in the cities, almost entirely among the lucky who have experienced the benefits of higher education and among parents who focus as much on their own and their partners' compatibility.

Although financial, social, and other pressures can cause a family to prefer an arranged path, 62% of its modern youth prefer marriage to a "lover or friend" as opposed to "casting a net." Only 36 percent agreed with the caste or community restrictions of their elders, while 65% completely disagreed, saying that, given the chance, they would marry a sweetie from another religion.

3.1. Arranged Marriages

In many cultures, the idea of romantic love is considered unnecessary when it comes to the relationship between two people who are looking to marry. Instead, families play an essential part in the match-making and becoming involved with the prospective life partner. Prior to the match-making tradition, it was more common that fathers (or a patriarchal figure) were responsible for choosing the suitor, but today the overall decision is more likely to be mutual between the bride and the groom. Arranged marriages that are initiated and planned by the union or the potential partners' families are generally chosen either for economic, social and/or cultural purposes – in other words, practical reasons. However, in many cases – especially in Western cultures – this is weird, uncommon and even cruel and the reaction often is: "Where is the love?"

As a matter of fact, a common, widespread stereotype in the Western cultural tradition is the perception of arranged marriages as "attacks against individualism and freedom". In other words, it is a violation of "us". Moreover, beliefs that individuals are forced into such relationships and have no freedom of choice may arise from cases known throughout the years - specifically those studied by older anthropologists. The truth is that a large proportion of subjects engaged in arranged marriages tend to continue rather having a lasting, loving, successful relationship with each other. For many decades now, scholars in the field have been researching this and similar issues to try and better understand other cultures. In an attempt to provide some clarity on the issue, this paper aims to answer the following question: How can one use knowledge about "non-Western" cultures and the social norms that exist within these societies to improve his/her own relationship(s)?

3.2. Filial Piety

When considering relationships in China, filial piety is an important concept to remember. Filial piety is a virtue of respect for one's parents, elders, and ancestors. It requires children to support, respect, and obey their parents and have a deep understanding of their family and heritage. This virtue is still very much alive with older generations and the idea of parents living in care homes is largely shunned. Many Chinese people believe that care homes represent rejection of one's duty to care for one's family. According to Marjolijn Bijlefeld and Sharon Krum, the Chinese "identify with their family, and the family is a very important concept."

In the United States, dating follows a traditional route. A romantic date is a custom with young people in urban areas; however, many traditions of courtship are not passed down among young people. In the United States, for people who are not going out with someone, "dating" can be romantic as well as allusive of 'hooking up' or 'spending time with someone.' In the United States, every culture has common dating customs, usually based on societal class, upbringing of the individual, religious beliefs, and social values. In the past, there is no changing (traditional) dating. It is not uncommon to date a woman for less than a year, in which the couple may decide to marry. The thought of being engaged but not living together is uncommon in the U.S. However, it is not unusual for a married couple to live together for a while prior to the big day.

3.3. Dowry and Bride Price

Dowry and bride price are both practices that are still performed in many places across the world. The definition of a dowry is something that women's families contribute towards the wedding, and traditionally, it is passed on in a lineage-type way when a woman gets married. In some cultures, the dowry is given to the couple as a wedding gift, but in others, it supports the bride in the marriage. Dowry practices still continue across the world, including in South Asia, the Middle East, and some African countries. A study found that we don't accept dowry in New Zealand through an application of in-depth qualitative research methods, although the researchers don't offer any explanation for how or why this can be so. Dowry is a practice that has been criticized as being oppressive to women and harmful to society. Often, women suffer from high dowry requirements due to the system of hypergamy, where women must marry in their same social group or higher.

Bride price, the practice of exchanging sums of money and gifts between the groom and the bride's family at marriage, occurs in different parts of Asia, sub-Saharan Africa, and in other parts of Africa. Archaeological records from as many as 2,000 years ago tell us that bride price is a well-established tradition. Bride price has been associated with negative outcomes for women, including violence, rape, and exploitation. A review of the practice of bride price as a driver of relationship violence found many studies that relate to it for different countries. Critics of bride price argue it enables men to buy a wife and daughters for trade for material gain. Critics argue that these practices perpetuate rigid gender roles, leading to women being objectified, and both domestic violence and infidelity being encouraged. The practices also can have serious negative consequences for women in terms of social, mental, and physical well-being. Ultimately, these practices contribute to reduced status for women and subordination to men.

CHAPTER 4

African Traditions

The Igbo people in the southeastern part of Nigeria are one of the ethnic groups that follow this tradition. There's one notable example in the southwest African Republic of Niger where the bride must walk to her husband's home – however far it may be – and carry a calabash filled with milk on her head. She kneels before her father-in-law and gives him some milk from the calabash, which symbolizes the bride's intention to care for her new family and a show of respect toward her in-laws. Amongst the Kukuyu of East Africa, it is tradition for the bride's uncle to play a key role during the ceremony. After the bride has been gifted to her husband, the bride places the leg of a proverbial 'stool of the ancestors' on the ground as an offering and an important gesture to ensure the families' ancestors will bless the marriage and produce children.

Great importance in many traditional African communities is placed on a couple's fertility and ability to produce children. In Nigeria, a couple who are unable to produce children are given the option to divorce by the husband's family, and the bride-price will be returned. Unfortunately, the same choice isn't available to the wife; her family is unable to return the dowry, and it's expected that she will stay with her husband until he is able to find a more fertile wife.

Africa is made up of 54 different countries with a diverse range of traditions, ethnicities, languages, and religious beliefs. It encompasses numerous different climates ranging from the desert to savannah to rainforests, which all have an impact on its inhabitants and the traditions they practice. Additionally, colonialism has left an impact on the traditions and languages in many African countries. These different factors have resulted in no one single date or type of traditional wedding being representative of all African wedding traditions. However, there are stories of actual weddings from around Africa that can give us a flavor of African wedding traditions. Here are 5 examples.

4.1. Polygamy and Polyamory

The following research uses the polygamous distribution identified by the anthropologist Bradford Wilcox as the most frequent in human populations to assess its influence on the very basis of the relative stability of power among these groups: human nature and modern social status.

In other words, for the majority of people, which of course had less immediate access to these same opportunities, increasing the number of men in relation to women until the average level of society became an evolutionary stable strategy. However, the abstract question remains: what role does the number of women and men, on the whole, play in the balance of power among human populations?

As the elite, in general, identified a strong link between intergenerational transmission of its status and the systematic availability of opportunities (private and public education, work for family and friends regimes) to its young people (men in particular), and does not value much the economies around this value, this custom lost interest through generations. This decrease in demand thus explains the gradual increase of monogamy up to its current use among the main population.

Recent studies offer decisive answers to doubts about the benefits of this custom and assistance to modern polyamory advocates. According to the scientific literature that suggests that polygamy was more beneficial for the elite than for the masses, few wives guarantee many children, which is not the case for many husbands. This rule was originally created to contain the incorporation of wealthy families whose wealth, through breeding, would be transformed into power by their descendants.

Many people believe that polygamous relationships, the practice of having more than one husband or wife at one time, are extremely rare, possibly resulting in a loose polyamory. However, polygamy was actually a more common practice than Western monogamous unions. This custom, reflected in the Bible, the Quran, the Constitution of the United Nations, and the majority of ancient legal codes, enigma scientists for many years.

4.2. Tribal Marriage Ceremonies

Because marriage ceremonies are official events, there's often a great deal of legalistic wrangling over the details, enforced by the headman of the trio. The wedding entitles the father-in-law to finally go and get his bride, long and prodigious litigation and negotiation once the son has indicated his intentions – usually years before the wedding. Such generosity serves to resolve any lingering sexual hostilities between the families by making divesting each other a near impossibility. There is much more to be said but suffice it to say that particular forms of social organization and indeed dietary practices are necessitated by the universal specificity of the marriage event among foragers. Every marriage society has its own recipe for mutually beneficial retail purchase and consumption/entebbe games.

Anthropologists have known for many years that the wedding ceremony is usually the most important event in the life of a tribal society. Among contemporary hunting-gathering tribes in the tropics, the fact that people are entering marriage can be confirmed from the raucous and protracted parties that often accompany the recruitment of a husband. The same event can signal the divorce of a couple (with the former wife moving to her mother's house).

4.3. Courtship Rituals

Bannister claimed that United States college students believe relationships serve the function of providing mutually stimulating and complimentary partners. Therefore, students utilize indirect strategies often to test if a desired partner would be both fun and qualified for a relationship. Negative behaviors, such as condescension, make a positive impact if they influence the partner's future behaviors and foster a sense of exclusivity by announcing a high bar. Intrusion after this turning point is self-confident, not highly conditional, truthful, sensitive, but still aggressive. In romantically involved United States students, both positive hypotheses of direct personal media (PM) behaviors, such as direct and positive non-playful teasing, and positive direct teasing PM behaviors, such as providing positive banter, increased with partner desirability. United States students also engage in and seem to value playful discourse in initializing hypotheses of PM behaviors that could be characterized as mild intrusiveness and secure displays of affection.

United States – In courtship rituals and conversational exchanges, Janet Bannister described techniques that college students use to entice a desirable person into a relationship. In the United States, college students often use humorous banter to engage in meaning negotiation and unlock positive confirmation from their partners. They also display positive affiliative verbal behaviors when pursuing desired relationships, such as providing positive facework and both direct and indirect compliments. Positive behaviors such as these generally receive favorable reactions from their partners.

CHAPTER 5

Middle Eastern Traditions

In Kurdistan, one of two regions in northern Iraq, fathers wear a special hat for a whole year when their daughter gets engaged. In the southern region of Iraq, when a woman marries she receives what is known as a "belly-plunging," an evening in her honor marked by laughter and a very specific dance - "the groom's belly dance." As soon as the festivities begin, men must arrive to interrupt the gathering, which surprises the newlyweds and disrupts the dance. This action mostly results in a good-natured exchange of money in order for the women to resume the music. Before the first dance between the bride and groom, one woman in particular - the best dancer - is given the chance to dance with the groom before he can begin the official first step. In the Gulf countries, marriage celebrations usually take place on Thursdays in order to allow for families coming from abroad to take part and for the celebration to take place until the early morning hours.

In Syria, wedding traditions are unique and individualized to every region. In the Lebanese town of Beirut, a sense of initiative distinguishes the betrothed couple, who are expected to plan the wedding and raise the funds to finance it. Most parents of the bride and groom refuse to get involved with the wedding except by offering moral support. This tradition - new for the country, but several decades old for the city - can sometimes go as far as forcing the betrothed to emigrate to avoid facing deep financial hardship and to marry as they wish. As for the Algerian town of Oran, after the fiancée finishes her henna evening, she will bring food to the neighboring houses. Upon entering, she calls on the residents to share in her happiness since her time as a single young woman is up. She marks her visit by smearing a little henna on the foreheads of the women who have come to meet her and to wish her well.

5.1. Islamic Marriage Practices

Islamic marriages have minimum requirements. A Muslim marriage is more or less a civil contract that normally does not require any ceremony. This contract might be arranged between the two parties with the following terms.

To a Muslim, Islam is a religion that is compatible with human nature and honors mankind above all other beings. There is full respect for both the natural obligations of the probable partner as well as the personal preferences the two parties would like to bring in. Fortunes have nothing to do with the acceptance of a partner, but only personal trustworthiness enables the two engaged parties to continue honoring the revered institution of marriage.

The most important requirement of a Muslim marriage on the side of the groom is to give a mahr to the bride. A mahr is owned by the bride only and must not be touched or used by anyone other than the concerned bride herself. During the lifetime of the bride, her family cannot request or take any of the mahr money owned by the bride. If the couple agrees, the amount of mahr can be relatively small. However, the mahr cannot be less than a nomadic gift level when the two groups cumulatively contribute their mahr to constitute the codein. Then, what defines the minimum limits of the mahr is the concerns and the financial positions of the two parties involved.

5.2. Henna Ceremonies

While the tradition of applying henna to a future bride is practiced in many cultures, from the Middle East and Mexico to India and Africa, some of the most beautiful of these ceremonies are in India and Pakistan. The bridal henna ceremony is often a private event held solely for the bride, her closest female friends and family members – and in a few cases, a professional henna artist. Tradition dictates that the henna – an herbal paste – must be applied on the evening before the wedding day. But while tradition often takes its course, contemporary henna ceremonies are a more flexible and growing trend amongst brides, with some holding it several days before the wedding to allow for alternatives to a full application, such as small tattoos, that come with an expiration date and don't have to wear off in time for the arrival of her new husband. Traditionally, henna is often applied to both the hands and the feet. Because the wedding night would be the first time that a groom would see his bride's body, he was offered the opportunity to find all the 'hidden names' that were worked into the intricate henna designs. In India, it's believed that the deeper and darker that the henna is, the more strongly that a daughter-in-law is loved by her husband and mother-in-law.

In addition to traditional observances, henna ceremonies have incorporated certain modern practices by incorporating symbols that could not traditionally be included, such as western wedding garments, rings and even specific designs – openly placing letters (or initials) of an intended loved one within the patterns that were created by the henna artist. The addition of these designs or text into henna is not typically recognized by traditional ceremonies, and in some regions, can be viewed as being quite controversial as the wedding ceremony is seen as a cultural and religious event already richly entrenched in imageries, symbolism, and cultural meanings. With growing acceptance in the West, the henna ceremony of India, the mehndi event, has seen an explosion in popularity of late. This has taken place not only on a personal level, but on a public level as well, through wedding websites, Indian wedding blogs, and the publication of magazines that describe how modern brides can include aspects of the mehndi ceremony as part of their westernized ceremony.

5.3. Modesty and Chaperoning

In Islamic and Middle Eastern cultures, in contrast to the Western notion of dating, even a physical involvement between a man and a woman comes after some type of engagement/marriage contract; it occurs within a framework of Western-structured courting. This courting involves four steps that culminate in marriage. First, the man sees the woman's face and converses with her. This may occur in a public place such as a café, or in her family's living room. If he then collects all his courage and competence and approaches her, she will remain silent to check if he is seeking her attention or simply exerting his masculinity. They then may start conversing, but the woman cannot give a word without being asked at that point. It should be noted that the Western notion of dating is not straightforward either: in Britain, its steps fit literally. Things in Britain occur at a similar pace, and while the woman needs to remain silent and reserved, the man may come more than once to the house asking questions and initiating the conversation.

Mahr is the second part of the marriage contract. In some Arab countries, women self-destate a 'bride price' which is given to them during their engagement from their future husbands. The mahr (dower), in Islam, is part of the marriage contract, and is not in exchange for marriage but in exchange for possible divorce as it serves as a protection for the woman, but also as a demonstration of consideration and respect from the husband. Unlike the Western engagement, the commitment formed by the components of the contract cannot be "shattered". The fiancée cannot be left, left waiting, or let alone, on the day of the wedding simply because the groom, other people, or things, get cold feet. Also, held in high honor, is the ideal of modesty, and a great emphasis is placed on that. Women need to be modest, and success in life or marriage depends on being so. Similarly in the Caucasus, African countries, the Philippines, and Japan, respect falls on the modest individuals and shows strongly through customs, traditions, and language. For example, modesty is significant in Chinese culture, where self-controlling and modest individuals intentionally relate to higher trustworthiness, greater inner tranquility, and emotional maturity.

CHAPTER 6

South American Traditions

A strong plant or a well-anchored mine-shaft: Brazil, Argentina, and Peru. The increasing individualism of Brazil has meant that, in many cases, there is a displacement of the responsibilities that used to rest on the family and the community onto the individual, who is then led to become more responsible as a citizen. In a similar way, the discomfort of living with a large number of people in close quarters in Brazil has led Brazilians to seek out knowledge of themselves as psychological beings capable of transforming the situation, an exploration that is being carried out, in great part, by women. In contrast to the men, who are less available for this inner exploration due to the pressures placed on them, the women feel the need to explore themselves because it is often through them that the transformations in living arrangements take place. The women are prepared to make the first move and transform their vision as a woman, a mother, and a human, taking up the roles that have been exclusively paternal until now, driven by the discomfort of being directed into situations that were not defined for them, each day in their quality as mothers.

On the other hand, there is no variation in the living arrangement of the women. Generally married to men who support all the changes, the women have a structural and emotional connection to the home in which the couple and the children live. This occurs because women are responsible for the home environment. Thus, when they enter into a loving relationship, women are looking for the stability of family life. This has led them to make great demands of their partners. A man who doesn't have a fixed monthly income or a high level of education, a well-regarded member of the community with a career and a clear future, stands little chance of charming a Brazilian woman. While these demands tend to propel women into less adventurous relationships, there is a predominance of well-balanced couples who embody a profound emotion.

6.1. Machismo and Marianismo

In Latin American cultures, machismo and marianismo are two of the most well-known trait stereotypes noticeably present in society. The beliefs and characteristics of machismo, mainly found in men, include "excellence, stoicism in the face of danger, self-assurance, independence, protectiveness of women, honor, forcefulness, aggressive behavior, and dominance." On the other hand, marianismo's traits, generally found in women, include "elevation of motherhood, purity, moral delicacy, martyrdom, self-sacrifice, emotional instability, submission to men, resilience, passivity, and nurturance." These two traits originated from an array of religious doctrines and the Spanish occupation of Latin America in the sixteenth century. In most, if not all, families with Latin American heritage, machismo and marianismo can be recognized. There is no "better approach" when referring to gender roles or stereotypes in families. However, in the 21st century, some families with Latin American heritage break from those norms to explore alternatives.

Relationships with their family and others outside of the family are extremely important since these families tend to surround themselves with extended family. The telenovelas have been the intimacy stimulants of choice and they engender more talk than soccer. Telenovelas have pervaded Latin American society since their inception in the 20s. Telenovelas provide everything one can think of: sex appeal, drama, conflict, and often a mix of action and historical drama. It masquerades the viewer with a fantasy, often romantic, but the storylines are built in reality, representation of real-life encounters: haves vs. have-nots, dueling families, lost or cursed heritage, forbidden love, or quest for identity. All are contained in any given telenovela. What is the consequence of this steadfast submission to a fantasy genre that reigns within the lives of the Latin community? It has been reported that Latin communities who watch telenovelas look to them as a moral code rather than entertainment.

6.2. Quinceañera Celebrations

In Mexico and some Central American cultures, such as Honduras, Guatemala, and El Salvador, the passage from girlhood to womanhood is celebrated on a girl's 15th birthday with a religious ceremony and a reception to follow. It's a grand affair, and she celebrates and dances with people who have supported her growing up. Balance bikes and Mini kick scooters are sometimes given to quinceañeras as a special gift. A festive meal is served, even in poor families. The religious festival as the formal celebration of a small girl's coming of age has Indian and Spanish roots, and it focuses on the girl's purity, humility, and modesty. Besides, faith, family, and community are a huge part of it. While those far from inner-city neighborhoods associated with poverty might not believe this applies anymore, certain versions of the ceremony are pretty narrow. The quinceañera tradition as known today is widely believed to have started in affluent circles of Mexico City as a way of expressing appreciation to God for seeing a daughter through to maturity. This kid is pretty common in Mexico; most girls have one. And this young lady to young woman change over a span of 5 years was profound. It was by far the most important event in many Mexican girls' lives.

The party starts as a formal entrance with a large and balanced honor court. After her big entrance, the attendants sit on stage for the ceremony, and each attests to a virtue or good deed, and maybe speaks or makes a gift presentation to her. There are numerous symbolic gestures where the mother or other important people in the girl's life, her godparents, grandmothers, and brothers all get a turn. Most mid to working-class Latinos I spoke with consider quinceañeras too expensive and risky — if much phenomena it had to be rich people's stuff they reasoned. While the US seems to be losing popularity of wasting money on 2 puffy dresses from early teenage years. Current would like to see the whole thing toned skippy but also bemoaned that girls want to show off that they're not a little kid anymore. I also spoke with Mexicans who felt strongly that the ceremony is very much alive and moving beyond its ugly ties to commercialism. It's true that a good deal of commercialism surrounds the day, but there are still deep traditional and real aspects of the tradition left.

6.3. Indigenous Relationship Customs

Australian Aborigines meet at ritual gatherings referred to as corroborees, at which day-to-day troubles are left outside. Young men attend with painted bodies; the women stand behind them, sheltered beneath large downy head feathers. The Bora of the American Indians is the name of many rituals held by small groups of boys and/or girls rotating over weeks, months, or years. They are held to prepare young people for adult roles, from initiation, the climax of the Bora, for which there may be one or many, to retirement as an elder. The initiation of Puberty ceremony, Walkabout, is perhaps more widely known than the Bora. Traditions varied dramatically by region, and an individual could participate in one, many, all—or none of the various customarily observed rituals.

When we engage in something that requires personal bravery, we can offer up a piece to the Spirits. The person must, after the successful outcome, discuss their action, asking for the aid of the Spirits that gave their piece and that still roam in and are a part of the land. In New Zealand, the Maori are the indigenous people. The Maori term that refers to traditional customs is tapu; the western connotation is sacred. Most aspects of Maori life are regulated by the tapu; for example, during ceremonies, men and women sit in separate rows while the kanohi ki te kanohi (face-to-face war challenge) is conducted. The Tapu association of sacred also warns against treading an individual's shadow upon another. While we do not engage in these customs of tomorrow's sense of today, it is perfectly acceptable to ask an individual to move out of your shadow, permitting you to retain the respect of the tapu. Visits to the sacred ground of your ancestors are a sign of respect; it is also a sign of disrespect when someone engages in this type of visit; care must be taken when amongst the remains of the ancestors.

CHAPTER 7

Asian Traditions

The Jewish tradition has a lovely way of fully recognizing the entrance or departure of a family member from the home. In movies, we often see people wave from the doorstep until their friend's car is out of view. But in Judaism, people stand under a "chuppah" - a special prayer shawl - as they say goodbye to their closest family members. This way, it's symbolic that you're with them as a support under the same cloth as long as you can be. Some also have a little cup of honey waiting for them to wipe their hand in, to show respect for difficult journeys coming and the sweetness of family when they return.

During the beautiful Hindu ladies' sangeet celebration before a wedding, both the bride and groom's families will create amazing costumes, skits, and musical masterpieces, celebrating the two who will become one the following day. It's a wonderful, bright, and happy way to create a bond between families before the wedding. It lasts a long time, and I can't imagine not learning to love these people after watching them dance for 4 hours. Some Hindu families also have a tradition of throwing newlyweds specific colors that mean health and cheerfulness, so that they will enter their life together full of brightness and happiness. Some of the brighter traditions for sure, and knowing it's been done for thousands of years makes it all the better.

Currying favor invites excess corruption, at least in China, or so they believe. So many have the modern tradition of burning a big pile of paper money at funerals to help bribe officials and give the dead a leg up in the ruling class. The elaborate fake money they burn is a familiar sight in funerals everywhere and has been common in China for at least 200 years!

7.1. Confucian Influence on Relationships

The Chinese culture, in particular, is rich in Confucian traditions. In Confucian ideology, the relationship between parents and children was considered to be the most fundamental of all human relationships. When Confucianism was adopted as the state ideology and had a great influence on politics and society, it was eventually established that marriage and the head of the family would be where the oldest son lived with his parents. These ideas became deeply rooted in people's minds, and many practices and thoughts related to families and relatives originated from this. It is said that the nuclear family and partitioned living did not become common in Japan or China until much later. Such customs are called "Confucian patterns," and they have had a strong influence on modern and contemporary people's lives.

There is a unique form of family called the xiao shun, which is exclusive to the Chinese culture and is a tradition rooted in Confucian thought. This tradition is similar to the subject of a previous study called a joint family in India. The term xiao shun consists of the character for "filial piety" and the character for "respect," and this form of family describes a family system that fosters harmony through generational respect and filial piety. In the xiao shun system, the oldest son is responsible for ensuring that the family members get along and all the assets and knowledge are passed on to the next generation. This oldest son offers ceaseless devotion to his parents as a form of filial piety.

7.2. Tea Ceremonies and Weddings

The oldest forms of wedding are reflected in the word "matrimony," which gives us the root for the word "mother," and gives an indication of why many marriages were arranged between families. In Europe, tradition calls for both bride and groom to wear lace, because the intertwining threads of lace signify their union. In Lithuania, it's been traditional to have a wedding well stocked with mead, beer and bread, with the expectation that the couple would take a ceremonial sip from a single cup. In other areas of Europe, using the sword to "cut" the wedding cake symbolizes the removal of obstacles to happiness in the couple's life.

Throughout Central Asia, traditional weddings include activities at several stages. Typically, the bride must first be won by the groom; he visits her home, where she gathers support from her relatives to beat him, and then when the woman takes pity on him, they are bound together. The bride is then taken in a luxurious procession accompanied by musicians performing traditional Central Asian melodies. "As soon as the bride is accepted into the groom's house, the groom's relatives savor the victorious performance and the young man's wit and dexterity." In Central Asia, the news of the wedding is usually quiet; the first congratulations come to the bride's relatives after the first child is born. From the moment of marriage, the wife takes on the responsibilities of her husband's family.

7.3. Concept of Face

This dimension was introduced by Professor H. B. Hwang. A significant part of Chinese philosophy of relationships is based on the Confucianism concept of "face". "Face" is an abstract concept where visibility of any person is available to others, but strangers do not see his/her "face". What is the "face"? This concept has a wide range of meanings and roles: it is like a social capital, like a value of a person from the point of view of the social circle to which a person belongs and the society as a whole. It is important for Chinese people to be good in social relations. A person is afraid to lose face in his relations with others. If it happens, it is very important to restore it very quickly. Though it is difficult to understand these concepts, taking no attention at them can lead to wrong interpretation of Chinese behavior and cultural distortions.

Chinese man tries not to "expose" (his face) in public, to show "face" of his interlocutor, to respect and esteem the cult of his reputation.

As for Chinese romantic relations, there are a lot of factors leading to the inequality of partners. Such relationship is closer to the model of traditional romantic relations, as they are understood in the western world. Despite the fact that the Chinese culture has a number of features, setting it apart from other cultures, according to these and many other principles, relations can have universal peculiarities that are typical cross-cultural. A couple can be viewed as just a pair, and there is usually no need to belong to any specific social circle. Many spouses have common interests and like to spend time together. Many marriages are created on the basis of love, but the process of obtaining permission from both of the families, unions of which are going to unite through their offspring, is compulsory. Every individual person has their own personal, unique perception of love.

CHAPTER 8

European Traditions

For nearly 300 years in Wales, a wood love spoon would be hand-crafted for the object of a young man's affections, along with patches of dogwood tree to signify his capabilities as a thrill-seeking leader, or intricate designs to represent their shared love. Spooning gifts were reciprocated on March 14 - Saint Valentine's Day, back on the Roman calendar until the Gregorian calendar (current international standard) took over and jettisoned 11 days in 1582. These unique, passionate objects are said to have held the status of an equivalent promise ring today. Often, love spoons have hearts, which in their own right signify generosity, request. If the courtee accepted the love spoon, the couple would solemnize their commitment and leave the neighborhood, becoming engaged. Eventually, only married couples would exchange love spoons, followed by the birth of their first child.

In Romania, on Feb. 24, Dragobete is the day when love does not sit still. Celebrating along with their lovebirds, Romanian couples and families walk amongst the villages and forests, and take part in the Dragobete customs and traditions. Youths pick flowers and elders hold ceremonial gatherings. Flower crowns signal unmarried women who wear them. Tapping another's sweetheart on the back with a snowdrop flower is said to lend them fair skin. Throughout the village, a jovial atmosphere is dutifully maintained.

8.1. Courtly Love

This definition was not lifelong. Courtly love maintained that courtly love was, by definition, a temporary form of love only readily fulfilled in the early stages of a man-woman romance - this is what is known by the French names of courtship or dating. Courtly love stories were told and retold in many different ways. One enduring theme, that 'love conquers all', sought to link the otherwise ignored interest in sexual relationships that were of primary importance in building up the social networks through marriage. For aristocratic families in late medieval and Renaissance Europe, it was important to set up love matches between their sons and daughters individually, based on matters of the heart, rather than have their husbands or the state arrange the marriage for political benefits as was previously the tradition. Young people had to be in control of matters of the heart because love, especially in a permanent form (marriage), would last longer and become a more dangerous emotion. Some historically important love stories depict the urgency to hide true feelings from an outside force, thus suggesting that the bond between the two lovers is cast from the same metal and possesses the capacity for mental, moral, and spiritual response.

Our contemporary idea of romantic love is often characterized by courtly love, which is tied to the chivalric knights of the Middle Ages. Elaborating on an idea that had been developing in oral and literary traditions from antiquity, courtly love was a medieval European conception of nobly and chivalrously expressing love and admiration. Generally, courtly love was defined as a secret, non-physical, moral relationship between a medieval chivalrous knight who might be married or unmarried, and a qualified noblewoman of high social status who was usually married and her husband would be absent. What the man was supposed to do is to guard the sanctity of his love and always defer to the maiden and pay homage to her. He showed his proud, manly independence and disdained the control of the love which attains his vision of 'perfect love' when he encounters the unutterable longings of the beloved merely with 'eternal love-longing' in himself.

8.2. Engagement Customs

Vietnam is another country where a civic wedding will not do. The traditional method for a man to marry in Vietnam includes a 3-step process. First, when the parents agree on the bride or groom, the groom-to-be is invited to dinner to meet the potential bride. If he is taken with her, he will formally request her hand in marriage from her parents. They will give him an answer soon after. Finally, the couple will hold a ban lon, "meaning widespread feast," wherein the couple will announce their intention to wed before all of their family and friends. When these 3 steps are complete, the wedding is considered legal in the eyes of the community.

When a man in Uganda wants to marry a woman, it's usually not just her heart that he needs to win. Traditionally, the suitor must present the bride's family with an engagement token in addition to the dowry. The traditional gift is an akawala, a reed woven into a regional mat. This custom symbolizes that the husband-to-be will be more than a partner to the woman but the very house she will call her home. Remember, Uganda is not a western country where all the children leave home when they grow up. Instead, like many traditional African customs, Ugandan families often live all together under the same roof!

8.3. Wedding Traditions

Some cultural presents will always be passed onto the bride's family by both the groom's family and the bride. In the past, this custom usually involved exchanging goods and the bride, but in the present day, some cultures have evolved this custom into a large dowry of money. The giving and receiving of a dowry operates as a social and economic arrangement. When both the groom and bride have contently given what is agreed upon, it signifies the free choice, mutual respect, and mutual commitment in their marriage union. In case of divorce or huge discontent between married couples, in most cases, the past dowry items come back to the original owners to be either destroyed, resold, or kept as mementos. Dowries are most common in South Asia, Africa, and Southeast Asia.

Whether planning a West versus an East wedding, weddings around the world share many common themes. For example, traditional wedding attire for a bride includes a white or very light-colored gown and a veil. Wedding attire for the groom includes a suit or tuxedo. Most weddings also involve the exchange of wedding bands between the bride and groom and a celebration afterwards with friends and family. In many cases, the father of the bride will also give a speech and a mother-son dance and father-daughter dance are also commonly seen at wedding receptions. In most non-Western cultures' weddings, there is also a heavy emphasis on a gift exchange, but their wedding attire and other traditions can be quite different from those we are more familiar with.

CHAPTER 9

Oceanic Traditions

Samoan weddings bring a whole new meaning to the term "wedding crasher". This is because it's actually tradition for the family of the groom to crash the wedding party of the bride. But wait, there's more! The groom's family is waiting too, meaning the bride's family will crash the wedding reception at the groom's house. This tug-of-war-like tradition symbolizes the family beginnings of the couple.

Traditional Fijian marriage is run by a "spokesperson" from the groom's family. Fijian weddings are concluded with the passing of the "Kalavata", a cultural object, from father to son. The fathers of the newlyweds previously passed it to the bride's parents. This tradition symbolizes the sharing of the family's knowledge and wisdom with the young couple. Also, the final decision on the wedding date is formally made by the sun, and by the groom's father's spokesman consulting the spirit world, ensuring the couple is forever blessed.

In Vanuatu, a tiny country in the South Pacific, a local tribe has a really odd custom, maybe the only one on this planet. They believe in the career of marriage brokers, in their own language called "nakamals". These marriage brokers are followed by the couple in the wild forest, the place where the Nakamals live and act. The couple dates for months around the places where the nakamals can be found. After they choose their brokers, the road to marriage is absolutely bizarre. They need to live together with the entire village for at least four years, sometimes even more. Four years of sacrifice in the name of love, living the cheap life, without basic facilities – it's a long and bumpy road to the altar. Once they pass this test, only then can the couple marry. The terrifying thing is the amount of time it takes Vanuatuans to eventually get married – always preceded by years of hardcore love scrutiny. Toss in family approval and the tribe, and you've got what we could call the longest first date in history.

9.1. *Maori Relationship Customs*

Due to the rich history and diverse nature of Maori culture, relationships and marriages of people from Maori descent often have unique customs that may or may not have been maintained throughout the centuries. As the culture of Maori was largely oral, it is difficult to determine how the customs may have changed. Equally, a great number of Maori and Pacific Island people have adopted a more European way of life, and these customs are less likely to be practiced. Despite these issues, it is clear that much matrimony amongst Maori families involves commitment to their traditional ways and customs, and these customs shape both the expectations of the couple and provide a framework that summarizes the roles of katoa within the marriage partnership, whether Maori or otherwise.

Requirements and obligations may also depend on the aspects of the cultures from both matenui when two people from diverse cultures marry, thereby adding other influences on the way married relationships are represented and maintained. Avoiding any of the traditional customs may also hold particular significance to the individuals of the metenui, especially when the blending of a specific tradition holds the significance of not only representing the Maori genealogy but also those of Pacific cultures. Such blending of customs indeed makes a 'traditional' approach unique, allowing greater relationships, especially when it is related to the greater cultural awareness that is now more prevalent.

9.2. Kinship Systems

Most societies throughout the world have systems of unilineal kinship; a special variant of a generational system that includes special roles for uncles, aunts, cousins, and grandparents. In contrast, anthropologists tend to be more impressed with the extreme complexity, rather than the great simplicity, of systems of cognatic kinship. Kin-types and grandparents are traced through all possible pathways available in the genealogical structure; any rule that permits an extension of kin can apply to either side. Moreover, genetic relatedness calculated by combining flows through both parents is the same as calculated for a plausible note of genetic relatedness, namely different pieces of connectedness derived by restricting flows to one parent at a time.

Symmetry around individuals (offspring of brother and sister have the same kinship types and dimensions of relatedness as those through brother and brother, or sister and sister) works well in the vast networks of interactions envisaged. Moreover, if we look away from simple systems of generational kinship, we find that all well-ordered systems are or may be represented as combinations of the two, dependent on cultural and ecological circumstances. Akin types are thus often highly evocative of relationships, but they sometimes also seem to reflect limited ways in which pairwise interactions interact in aggregate; parents of spouses are 'parents-in-law' – essentially a double counting of the fact that each party is parent of their own spouse.

9.3. Sacred Love Stories

Sacred Love Stories: In my many travels around the world, I have encountered a number of shared mythologies and love stories that stood out to me. Although numerous variations of these love stories exist, all cultures think of their own version as the original and regard it to be the purity of true and natural love.

In Southeast Asia, the sacred love story of Rama and Sita comes from Indian mythology. When I was in Balinese theater, instead of actual movies, stalls could only offer films showing Balinese shadow puppet shows and Rama and Sita's adventures. Every evening, everyone would gather together to watch Rama's and Sita's exciting epic and dreamily sigh about each beautiful act. As a man from the village would recite the story in song, the sound of his voice would resonate with the guests' emotions. When Rama and Sita were in danger, every heart beat faster, and when they faced crises, the guests' breathing acoustically synched into suspense. A part of me also sank into the characters' emotions. By the time the show was over, my eyes shone with tears.

In Peru, it is the legend of Manco Cápac and Mama Ocllo. Peruvian mythology believes that the first ancestor of the Incas, a sun god, had descended to earth and emerged from the waters of Lake Titicaca. One day, Manco Cápac had been exploring the area and found Mama Ocllo. She was weaving a large bed of grain and singing a prayer to the moon. Manco Captain was moved by her melodies and decided to become her partner in life. The sun god told them to travel together, carry gold rods, and seek a land that will be resplendent and prosperous. The love of the first Inca for his sister-wife made the nation that legends have since been built upon. The Incas' royal tradition had also been demonstrated by inter-marriages between fictional descendants of this mythological couple to preserve and expand wealth.

CHAPTER 10

Conclusion

Over the last 10 sections, we've taken a pretty epic trip around the world. I've bulldozed through a smidge under 50 countries worth of "first date" customs, and we've checked out the ins and outs of engagement, weddings, anniversaries, and even sappy little love customs involving flowers, hearts, and, yes, even double-barreled shotguns. We have ploughed through more terrae that an Englishman in search of more, well, terrâ, so even I am fully ready to wrap this thing up with a little heartfelt conclusion.

Why? Well, because nothing - ladies, guys, sisters, brothers, friends, Romans, countrymen and anyone else - is more heartwarming, cute, fuzzy, or - yes - lovely than a true, enveloping love that engulfs and warms the lives of everyone it touches. I really mean that too. Call me a sop, a scoff or whatever else you fancy, but for this little blokey, nothing says life, health, soul or spirit more than seeing people who, with that radiant, positive bond, lift themselves, their friends, their family and all those around them up into heights they never before knew, felt or imagined. Wow.

Milton Keynes UK
Ingram Content Group UK Ltd.
UKHW040329031224
452051UK00011B/323